LET'S LEARN ABOUT
COMPUTER SCIENCE

NETWORKS

Jeff Mapua

Enslow Publishing
101 W. 23rd Street
Suite 240
New York, NY 10011
USA

enslow.com

WORDS TO KNOW

cable Electrical wires in a bundle around a main core.

data Information that is used in a computer.

hardware The parts of a computer system that you can touch.

local area network (LAN) A network that connects computers in a building or small area.

network Computers and equipment that are connected to each other.

node A computer or machine that is part of a network.

personal area network (PAN) One person's network. It may have computers, phones, and tablets.

wide area network (WAN) A network connecting computers that may be far apart.

wireless Not using cables or wires.

worldwide Throughout the world.

CONTENTS

Computers that work together are called a network.

What Is a Network?

Many people use only one computer. But sometimes computers are connected to other computers and **hardware**. When computers are connected, it is called a **network**.

FAST FACT

The word "network" is from the 1550s.

A network is like a spider's web. All of the different parts connect to each other.

Nodes

Networks can have more than just computers. Networks can also connect printers, phones, and other equipment. A machine on the network is called a **node**.

FAST FACT

A router is a machine that helps move information between nodes on a network.

This network cable
runs along the
bottom of the ocean.

Connections

How are computers connected? A network may use wires or **cables**. These can be miles long. Networks today use radio signals, too. These networks are **wireless**.

FAST FACT

Network cables can be placed at the bottom of the ocean. Sharks sometimes bite them!

Computer networks are an easy way for people to talk to each other.

What Networks Share

Nodes "talk" to each other. They send **data** through the network. People can use networks to share files. They can also talk to one another.

FAST FACT

Networks that are used in an office help people work together.

Networks can connect computers all over a city.

Types of Networks

There are different kinds of networks. They are different because of their size. A **personal area network** connects one person's machines. Other networks connect countries with each other.

FAST FACT

Networks can connect to other networks. Together they make an even bigger network.

Students use computer networks in schools.

LAN

A **local area network** connects computers in one place. They can be in offices, homes, and schools. A local area network is called a LAN for short.

FAST FACT

Computers on a LAN can use the same printer.

Some networks reach all across the world.

WAN

Networks can connect cities, states, or even countries. These networks cover a wide area. They are called a **wide area network**. We call them WAN for short.

Fast Fact

Computers on a WAN can connect to each other without using wires.

The World Wide Web helps people use the internet.

The Internet

The most popular network in the world is called the internet. It is a **worldwide** computer network. It connects countries around the world.

FAST FACT

The internet and World Wide Web are two different things. The Web is a way to use the internet's network of computers.

The internet is a huge network that connects computers around the world.

Biggest Network in the World

The internet changed the world. People can do many things online. They can shop and play games. The internet connects millions of computers around the world.

FAST FACT

More than three billion people use the internet.

Activity
Fun with Networks

MATERIALS
paper
pencil

Want to learn more about networks? Try this activity:

Figure out your "personal network." Write down your name on a large sheet of paper.

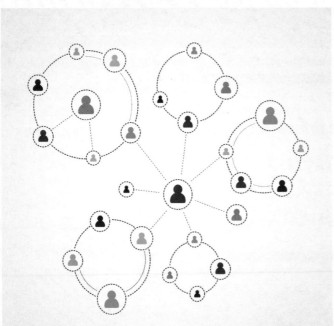

Write down names of your friends and family. Group people based on how they are related to you or how you know them.

Write down the names of friends and family members of the people in your network. See how many connections you can make!

LEARN MORE

Books

Gifford, Clive. *Computer Networks.* New York, NY: Crabtree, 2015.

Linde, Barbara M. *Computer Network Architect.* New York, NY: PowerKids Press, 2017.

Reed, Jennifer. *What Are Computer Networks and the Internet?* New York, NY: Britannica, 2018.

Websites

CS Unplugged

csunplugged.org / network-protocols
Find out more about computer networks. Activities to help understand computer basics are available.

PBS LearningMedia

ca.pbslearningmedia.org / resource / ate10.sci. engin.design.networks / computer-networks
Learn more about computer networks, how they talk to one another, and the different types of networks.

INDEX

Published in 2019 by Enslow Publishing, LLC.
101 W. 23rd Street, Suite 240, New York, NY 10011

Library of Congress Cataloging-in-Publication Data

Names: Mapua, Jeff, author.
Title: Networks / Jeff Mapua.
Description: New York, NY: Enslow Publishing, LLC, 2019. | Series: Let's learn about computer science | Includes bibliographical references and index. | Audience: Grades K to 4.
Identifiers: LCCN 2018004907| ISBN 9781978501836 (library bound) | ISBN 9781978502291 (pbk.) | ISBN 9781978502307 (6 pack)
Subjects: LCSH: Computer networks—Juvenile literature.
Classification: LCC TK5105.5 .M3584 2019 | DDC 004.6—dc23
LC record available at https://lccn.loc.gov/2018004907

Printed in the United States of America

To Our Readers: We have done our best to make sure all website addresses in this book were active and appropriate when we went to press. However, the author and the publisher have no control over and assume no liability for the material available on those websites or on any websites they may link to. Any comments or suggestions can be sent by e-mail to customerservice@enslow.com.

Photos Credits: Cover, p. 1 wavebreakmedia/Shutterstock. com; pp. 2, 3, 24 Best-Backgrounds/Shutterstock.com; p. 4 Bildagentur Zoonar GmbH/Shutterstock.com; p. 6 Petekub/Shutterstock.com; p. 8 ton koene/Alamy Stock Photo; p. 10 Andrey_Popov/Shutterstock.com; p. 12 jamesteohart/Shutterstock.com; p. 14 Tyler Olson/Shutterstock.com; p. 16 Toria/Shutterstock.com; p. 18 Georgejmclittle/Shutterstock. com; p. 20 Anton Balazh/Shutterstock.com; p. 22 Mert Toker/Shutterstock.com; interior design elements (laptop) ArthurStock/Shutterstock.com, (flat screen computer) Aleksandrs Bondars/Shutterstock.com.